I0484789

ACCOUNTANCY

PART-3

:: Author ::

ROBIN N. VORA

(M.COM., B.ED., SLET)
GUJARAT UNIVERSITY RANKER

PUBLISHED BY

The New Era International Publishing House
HQ. At & Po. Chaveli., Ta- Chansma,
Dist- Patan, North Gujarat, India, Asia.

First Publication: 5th FEBRUARY, 2015

Copyright: Author
(c) ROBIN N. VORA

ISBN:- 978-15-08472-70-4

Price: Rs.750/- INDIA
$ 15 OUTSIDE INDIA

PUBLISHED BY

The New Era International Publishing House
HQ. At & Po. Chaveli., Ta- Chansma,
Dist- Patan, North Gujarat, India, Asia.

Dedicated
to
my
Parents

INDEX

CHAPTER – 1

("ADMISSION OF A NEW PARTNER")

📋 IMPORTANT POINTS 📋

a) The determination of new profit sharing ratio

1) When profit sharing ratio of old partners and share of new partners are specified :
- $\Rightarrow$ Assume that total profit = **1**
- $\Rightarrow$ Remaining share of profit = Total profit – Share of new partner in profit
- $\Rightarrow$ New share = Remaining share $\times$ Old Ratio

2) When sacrificed share of Old partners is specified :

♣ New Ratio = Old Ratio – Sacrificed share

3) When proportion of Sacrificed share by Old partners is specified :
- ➤ Sacrificed share by Old partners = share of new partner in profit $\times$ proportion of Sacrificed
- ➤ New share = Remaining share $\times$ Old Ratio

4) *When Sacrificed share of some partners are specified and Sacrificed share of One partner is not specified :*

✦ *Sacrificed share of Old partner (Whose sacrificed share is not given) = Share of New partner in profit − Sacrificed share of Old partner (Whose sacrificed share is given)*

✦ *New Ratio = Old Ratio − Sacrificed share*

5) *When Old partners Sacrificed certain share in favour of new partner from their profit and share of new partner in profit is not specified :*

✓ *Sacrifice of Old partner = Ratio of Old partner ✗ proportion of his own share Sacrificed in favour of new partner*

✓ *New Partner's share in profit = Total of Sacrificed share of Old Partners (Eg. Sacrificed share of A + Sacrificed share of B)*

✓ *New Ratio = Old Ratio − Sacrificed share*

b) *The calculation of Sacrificed share of Old Partners*
Sacrificing Ratio = Old Ratio − New Ratio

c) *Goodwill and Its Accounting Effects :*
1) *Premium Method :*

This method is followed when the new partner pays his share of goodwill in cash. The amount of premium brought in by the new partner is shared by the existing partners in their ratio of sacrifice.If this amount is paid to the old partners directly (privately) by the new partner, no entry is made in the books of the firm. But, when the amount is paid through the firm, which is generally the case, the following journal entries are passed :

Cash A/c   Dr. *(Share of new Partner of total value of goodwill)*

      To Old Partners Capital A/c

(In Sacrificing Ratio)

OR

Alternative Method :

(i) Cash/ Bank A/c   Dr.

      To Goodwill A/c

(Amount brought by new partner as premium)

(ii) Goodwill A/c   Dr.

      To Old Partners Capital A/c (Individually)

(Goodwill distributed among the existing partners in their sacrificing ratio)

Note : If the any of the Old Partner or Both Partners withdraw part or full amount of their goodwill :

Old Partners Capital A/c   Dr.

     To Cash / Bank A/c

♣ *Goodwill Revaluation Method :*

When Goodwill Account is not there in the books of Partnership firm :

For creating Goodwill Account

   Goodwill A/c   Dr. (Total value of Goodwill)
    To Old Partners Capital A/c (Old Ratio)

For write off Goodwill Account

All Partners Capital A/c (Including New Partner) Dr
 To Goodwill A/c (New Ratio) (Total value of Goodwill)

i.   *When Goodwill Account is there in the books of Partnership firm :*

 ♣ *When new value of goodwill determined is similar to disclosed value of goodwill.*

- *No entry*

 ♣ **When New Value of Goodwill is Determined More than the Disclosed Value of Goodwill :**

- **When new value of Goodwill is determined more than the disclosed value of Goodwill at the time of partner Z is admitted : (In Old Ratio and Difference between new value of Goodwill and Old value of Goodwill)**

Date	Particulars	Debit	Credit
1/4/2012	Goodwill A/c Dr. To X's capital a/c To Y's capital a/c To Z's capital a/c		

♣ *When new Value of Goodwill is determined less than disclosed value of Goodwill :*

- *When new value of Goodwill is determined less than the disclosed value of Goodwill at the time of partner Z is admitted : (In Old Ratio and Difference between old value of Goodwill and new value of Goodwill)*

Date	Particulars	Debit	Credit
1/4/2012	X's capital a/c Dr. Y's capital a/c Dr. Z's capital a/c Dr. To Goodwill a/c		

Note : When Goodwill A/c will be written off at that time Partners Capital A/c (Including New Partner)will be debited and Goodwill A/c will be credited. (In New Ratio)

☐ THEORY SECTION ☐

A new partner can be admitted in an on existing partnership firm in two ways as per partnership act as follows :

> *If all existing partners decide unanimously to admit a new partner.*
> *If there is a provision in the partnership agreement for admission of a new partner.*

❖ **Reasons for admitting a new partner :**

i. *When existing partnership firm needs additional capital.*

ii. *When existing partnership firm needs additional working capacity.*

iii. *When any partners retirement or death, admission of a new partner takes place.*

iv. *To sustain the existence of a skilled and efficient employee of the firm with this intention making him partner.*

⇒ *Following are the other important points which require attention at the time of admission of a new partner:*

1. *New profit sharing ratio;*
2. *Sacrificing ratio;*
3. *Valuation and adjustment of goodwill;*

4. Revaluation of assets and Reassessment of liabilities;

5. Distribution of accumulated profits (reserves); and Adjustment of partners' capitals.

☐ PRACTICAL SECTION ☐

1. Anita and Vishal are partners sharing profits in the ratio of **1:2**. They admitted Sumit as a new partner for **1/5** share in the future profits of the firm. Calculate new profit sharing ratio of Anita, Vishal and Sumit.

2. Ram and Shyam are partners in a firm sharing profits in the ratio of **3:2**. They admit Ghanshyam as a new partner. Ram surrenders **1/4th** of his share and Shyam **1/3** of his share in favour of Ghanshyam. Calculate new profit sharing ratio of Ram, Shyam and Ghanshyam.

3. Amar and Bahadur are partners in a firm sharing profits in the ratio of **3:2**. They admitted Marry as a new partner for **1/4th** share. Marry would receive his share from Amar and Bahadur in the ratio of **2:1**. Calculate new profit sharing ratio.

4. Anil and Mukesh are partners in a firm sharing profits in the ratio of **7:5**. They admitted Ratan as a new partner for **2/8th** share in the profits, for which Ratan would receive **2/8th** share from Anil and **1/8th** share from Mukesh. Calculate new profit sharing ratio of Anil, Mukesh and Ratan.

5. **H.L**. and **J.G.** are partners in a firm Sharing profits in the ratio of **2:5**. They admitted **L.J.** as a new partner for **1/5th**

share. **L.J.** would receive *1/10th* his share from **H.L.** and remaining part from **J.G.** Calculate new profit sharing ratio.

6. Sunil and Dalip are partners in a firm sharing profits and losses in the ratio of **5:3**. Sachin is admitted in the firm for *1/5th* share of profits. He is to bring in **Rs.20,000** as capital and **Rs.4,000** as his share of goodwill.

   Give the necessary journal entries,

   (a) When the amount of goodwill is retained in the business

   (b) When the amount of goodwill is fully withdrawn.

   (c) When **50%** of the amount of goodwill is fully withdrawn

7. Vijay and Sanjay are partners in a firm sharing profits and losses in the ratio of **3:2**. They decide to admit Ajay into partnership with **1/4** share in profits. Ajay brings in **Rs.30,000** for capital and there quisite amount of premium in cash. The goodwill of the firm is valued at **Rs.20,000**. The new profit sharingratio is **2:1:1**.Vijay and Sanjay withdraw their share of goodwill.

   Give necessary journal entries.

8. Ahuja and Shah are partners in a firm sharing profits and losses in the ratio of **3:2**. They decide to admit Chaudhary into partnership for **1/5** share of profits,which he acquires equally from Ahuja and Shah.Goodwill is valued at **Rs.30,000**.

   Chaudhary brings in **Rs.16,000** as his capital but is not in aposition to bring any amount for goodwill. No goodwill account exists in booksof the firm. Goodwill account is to be raised at full value. Record the necessary journal entries.

9. *Raina and Rahim are partners in a firm sharing profits and losses in the ratio of **1:4**. Rahul is admitted into partnership for **1/3** share in profits. He brings in **Rs.10,000** as capital, but is not in a position to bring any amount for his share of goodwill which has been valued at **Rs.30,000**.*

Give necessary journal entries under each of the following situations:

   (a)   *When there is no goodwill appearing in the books of the firm;*

   (b)   *When the goodwill appears at **Rs.15,000** in the books of the firm; and*

   (c)   *When the goodwill appears at **Rs.36,000** in the books of the firm.*

10.   *Following in Balance Sheet of A and B who share profits in the ratio of **4:1**.*

   *Balance Sheet of A and B as on April **1, 2009***

Liabilities		Amount Rs.	Assets	Amount Rs.
Capital :			Plant & Machinery	30,000
A :	30,000		Furniture	15,000
B :	20,000	50,000	Stock	10,000
Creditors		20,000	Debtors	12,000
			Cash balance	3,000
		70,000		70,000

   On that date C is admitted into the partnership on the follo wing terms:

1) *C is to bring in **Rs.15,000** as capital and **Rs.5,000** as premium for goodwill for **1/6** share.*

2) *The value of stock is reduced by **10%** while plant and machinery is appreciated by **10%**.*

3) *Furniture is revalued at **Rs.9,000**.*

4) *A provision for doubtful debts is to be created on sundry debtors at **5%** and **Rs.200** is to be provided for an electricity bill.*

5) *Investment worth **Rs.1,000** (not mentioned in the balance sheet) is to be taken into account.*

6) *A creditor of **Rs.100** is not likely to claim his money and is to be written off.*

Record journal entries and prepare revaluation account and capital account of partners.

11. *BOI and BOB are partners of a firm sharing profit and loss ratio of **4:1** The balance sheet of their firm as on **31-3-2012** is as under :*

Balance Sheet as on 31-3-2012

Liabilities	Amount Rs.	Asset	Amount Rs.
Capital Accounts :		Machines	52,500
BOI– 1,50,000		Land & Building	1,35,000
BOB– 75,000	2,25,000	Furniture	45,000
Current Accounts :		Stock	37,500
BOI – 22,500		Debtors 31,500	
BOB – 7,500	30,000	– Bad debts 1,500	

Workmen profit sharing fund	4,500	30,000	
Workmen compensation fund	18,000	– Bad debts reserve 3,000	27,000
Creditors	22,500	Bills receivable	9,000
Bank overdraft	15,000	Cash Balance	3,000
		Outstanding income	6,000
	3,15,000		3,15,000

On the date of balance sheet, they admitted SBI as a new partner on the following terms :

❖ SBI should bring in **Rs.1,12,500** towards her capital and **Rs.27,000** towards her ¼ share in goodwill. Half the amount of goodwill will be withdrawn by old partners immediately.

❖ Land and building to be appreciated by **10 %.**

❖ Furniture and stock to be reduced by **5%.**

❖ Provide **7.5 %** for **BDR** on debtors.

❖ Outstanding salary of **Rs.500** to be recorded in the books.

❖ The claim of **Rs.2000** towards workmen accident compensation fund is admitted but not yet recorded.

From the above information, prepare necessary accounts and Balance sheet after the admission of a new partner.

12. *Abhishek and Aishwarya are partners of a partnership firm sharing profit and loss in equal proportion. The balance sheet of their firm as on* **30 - 6 - 2011** *is as under :*

Balance sheet as on 30-6-2011

Liabilities	Rs.	Asset	Rs.
Capital Account		Land- building	1,12,500
Abhishek : 78,750		Debtors 24,750	
Aishwarya : 56,250	1,35,000	−BDR 2,250	22,500
Creditors	24,750	Stock	40,500
Other liabilities	20,250	Cash balance	4,500
	1,80,000		1,80,000

On the date of balance sheet, Abhishek and Aishwarya admitted Aaradhya as a new partner in partnership on the following terms :

❖ *Aaradhya should bring* **Rs.56,250** *in cash as capital against his ¼th share in future. The value of goodwill is determined at* **Rs.22,500.**

❖ *Aaradhya is not able to bring his share of goodwill in cash. Partners have decided not to disclose goodwill at its full value.*

❖ *The value of Land-building is determined at* **Rs.1,20,000.**

❖ *Provide* **10 %** *for* **BDR** *on debtors.*

❖ *Outstanding income is of* **Rs.5,000.**

❖ *The value of stock is to be reduced by* **Rs.3,500.**

❖ *Out of total creditors* **Rs.2,000** *now are not payable.*

❖ *Partners decide to show assets and liabilities at old value after admission of a new partner.*

From the above information, if partners decide to show assets and liabilities at old value after the admission of a new partner, then prepare the new balance sheet along with necessary accounts.

13. *Mobile and Pager are partners of a partnership firm sharing profit and loss in the ratio of 6:3. The balance sheet of their firms as on 31-3-2011 is as under :*

Balance Sheet as on 31-3-2011

Liabilities	Amount Rs.	Asset	Amount Rs.
Capital Accounts :		Goodwill	4,500
Mobile : 50,000		Land	50,000
Pager : 50,000	1,00,000	Building	25,000
P & L a/c	4,500	Machines	30,000
Creditors	15,000	Debtors	10,000
Bills Payable	5,000	Bills receivable	5,000
Unpaid salary	2,500	Cash Balance	2500
	1,27,000		1,27,000

On the above balance sheet, they admitted a new partner Cordless to give 1/5ᵗʰ share in profit on the following conditions :

❖ *Cordless should bring capital of Rs.35,000 in cash.*

❖ *New value of goodwill is determined at **Rs.7,500** and to be disclosed in the books.*

❖ *The New value of land is **Rs.60,000**.*

❖ *The value of Building is to be reduced by **Rs.1400**.*

❖ *The market value of Machines **Rs.27,500**.*

❖ *Provide **10 %** for **BDR** on debtors.*

❖ *From creditors **Rs.750** now are not payable.*

❖ *Cordless would receive his share from Mobile and Pager in the ratio of **3:2**.*

From the above information, prepare necessary accounts and balance sheet in the books of firm.

14. **P** and **Q** are partners of a firm sharing profit and loss in **2:1** proportion. They have admitted **R** to give ¼ share in profit. R has to bring his capital in cash, Which is ¼ of the net assets of the new firm. After giving the effects of all accounting adjustments, the capital of **P** and **Q** is arrived at **Rs.70,000** and **Rs. 25,000** respectively. Find the capital brought in by **R**.

🗍 LATEST EXAMINATION 🗍

---

15. *Karan and Kiran are partners of a partnership firm sharing profit in the ratio **3:2**. The balance sheet of their partnership firm as on **31-03-08** is as under.*

Balance sheet as on **31-03-08**

Liabilities	Rs.	Assets	Rs.
Capital :		Land	5,50,000
Karan : **6,00,000**		Building	2,20,000
Kiran : **4,00,000**	**10,00,000**	Machines	2,00,000
Creditors	**50,000**	Stock	40,000
Bills payable	**30,000**	Debtors	60,000
Outstanding expenses	**40,000**	Bills receivable	10,000
		Bank balance	15,000
		Cash balance	15,000
		P & L A/c (Debit)	10,000
	11,20,000		**11,20,000**

On balance sheet date, Kanan is admitted to give ¼ share with the following conditions.

1. Kanan will bring capital of **Rs.2,50,000** in cash and **Rs.10,000** as his share of goodwill.

2. To increase the value of land and building by **Rs.30,000** and **Rs.10,000** respectively.

3. To record market value of **Rs.1,30,000** for machines in the books.

4. To reduce the value of stock by **10 %**.

5. To provide **5%** for bad debts reserve and **2%** discount reserve on debtors.

6. Out of creditors **Rs.5,500** are now not payable.

7. Unrecorded unpaid liability is of **Rs.2,500**. Unrecorded insurance premium paid in advance is **Rs.1,000**.

From the above information pass necessary journal entries and prepare Revaluation account, Partner's Capital accounts, and Balance Sheet after admission of Kanan in the books of the firm.

(March,09)

16. Kolavari and Godavari are partners of a partnership firm sharing profit in the **2:1**. The balance sheet of their partnership firm as on **31-03-10** is as under.

Liabilities	Rs.	Assets	Rs.
Capital :		Land	3,00,000
Kolavari : **2,00,000**		Building	1,00,000
Godavari : **3,00,000**	5,00,000	Goodwill	54,000
Profit and loss account	18,000	Stock	40,000
General reserve	30,000	Debtors	60,000
Creditors	50,000	Bills receivable	20,000
Bills payable	16,000	Cash/Bank balance	40,000
	6,14,000		6,14,000

On balance sheet date, Maheshvari is admitted to give 1/5 share with the following conditions.

➤ Maheshvari should bring capital of **Rs.1,60,000** in cash.
➤ New value of goodwill is determined at **Rs.72,000** and to be disclosed in the books.
➤ The value of the Land and Building is to be increased by **10%**.
➤ The value of the stock is to be reduced by **Rs.8,000**.

➤ *Provide 5% BDR on debtors.*
➤ *From creditors Rs.40,000 are not payable.*
➤ *New profit and loss sharing ratio is determined at 1:3:1.*

From the above information prepare necessary accounts and Balance Sheet in the books of the firm.

(March,10)

17. *Sachin and Saurav are partners of a partnership firm sharing profit in the equal proportion . The balance sheet of their partnership firm as on 31-03-11 is as under.*

Balance sheet as on 31-03-11

Liabilities	Amount Rs.	Assets	Amount Rs.
Capital :		Land & Building	1,00,000
Sachin : 1,00,000		Plant	50,000
Saurav : 1,00,000	2,00,000	Investments	50,000
Creditors	17,500	Stock	5,000
General reserve	7,500	Debtors 16,500	
		– BDR 1,500	15,000
		Cash & Bank balance	5,000
	2,25,000		2,25,000

On the same date, Rahul is admitted to give 1/5 share with the following conditions.

1. *Rahul would bring Rs.75,000 as capital.*
2. *Land & Building valued at Rs.1,50,000.*
3. *The value of Plant is to be increased by Rs.10,000.*
4. *Investment valued at Rs.40,000.*
5. *Provide 10% for bad debts reserve on debtors.*

6. Out of creditors **Rs.875** are not required to pay.

(March,11)

18. Sameer and Neeraj are partners of a partnership firm sharing profit in the **1:2**. The balance sheet of their partnership firm as on **31-03-09** is as under. **(March,12)**

Liabilities	Amount Rs.	Assets	Amount Rs.
Capital :		Land	1,50,000
Sameer : **1,00,000**		Building	50,000
Neeraj : **1,50,000**	**2,50,000**	Goodwill	27,000
Profit and loss account	**9,000**	Stock	20,000
General reserve	**15,000**	Debtors	30,000
Creditors	**25,000**	Bills receivable	10,000
Bills payable	**8,000**	Cash/Bank balance	20,000
	3,07,000		**3,07,000**

On balance sheet date, Vikram is admitted to give **1/5** share with the following conditions.

➢ Vikram should bring capital of **Rs.80,000** in cash.
➢ New value of goodwill is determined at **Rs.36,000** and partners decide not to be disclose value of goodwill in the books.
➢ The value of the Land and Building is to be increased by **10%**.
➢ The value of the stock is to be reduced by **20%**.
➢ Provide **5%** BDR on debtors.

➢ *From creditors **Rs.5,000** are not payable.*

➢ *Vikram would receive his share from Sameer and Neeraj in the ratio of **2:1**.*

From the above information prepare necessary accounts and Balance Sheet in the books of the firm.

19. *Vishal and Jigar are partners of a partnership firm sharing profit and loss in the equal ratio.*

Liabilities		Rs.	Assets	Rs.
Capital			Land & Building	50,000
Vishal :	60,000		Machines	30,000
Jigar :	30,000	90,000	Stock	4,000
Creditors		5,000	Debtors	6,000
P & L A/c		2,000	Cash balance	10,000
General Reserve		3,000	Bills receivable	20,000
Bills Payable		20,000		
		1,20,000		1,20,000

On the balance sheet, date they admitted Sagar on the following condition :

1) *Sagar would bring capital equal to his share in the firm and **Rs.6,000** in cash towards goodwill.*

2) *New profit and loss sharing ratio is determined at **3:2:1**.*

3) *Market value of land & Building is **Rs.48,000** whilt market value of machines is **Rs.34,000**.*

4) *Salary outstanding its **Rs.1,500**.*

5) *Outstanding income of* **Rs.500** *is to be recorded.*

From the above information, prepare necessary accounts and new balance sheet in the books of the firm. Show all calculation as a part of the answers.

(March,13)

20. *Chingu and Mingu are partners of a partnership firm sharing profit and loss in the proportion of* **2:3.**

Balance Sheet as on 31-12-2009

Liabilities	Rs.	Assets	Rs.
Capital		Land & Building	60,000
Chingu : 30,000		Machines	10,000
Mingu : 50,000	80,000	Stock	10,000
Creditors	12,000	Debtors	15,000
General Reserve	8,000	Cash balance	3,000
		P & L A/c	2,000
	1,00,000		1,00,000

On the above mentioned date, they admitted Thingu in their partnership on the following conditions:

1) *Thingu would bring necessary amount towards capital on the basis of her profit and loss ratio and* **Rs.5,000** *in cash towards goodwill.*

2) *New profit and loss sharing ratio is determined at* **2:2:1.**

3) *The value of land and building is to be increased by* **Rs.10,000** *and consider the value of machine at* **Rs.12,000.**

4) *Provide* **10%** *for* **BDR** *on debtors.*

5) *Outstanding income not recorded is* **Rs.1,000.**

From the above information show all calculation and prepare accounts and new balance sheet in the books of the company. **(March,14)**

.............×××××××××.........

CHAPTER – 2

(*"RETIREMENT OR DEATH OF A PARTNER"*)

⌐ IMPORTANT POINTS ⌐

Normally, the continuing partners acquire the share of retiringor deceased partners in the old profit sharing ratio, and there is no need to compute the new profit sharing ratio among them,as it will be same as the old profit sharing ratio among them. In fact, in the absence of any information regarding profit sharing ratio in which the remaining partners acquire the share of retiring/deceased partner, it is assumed that they will acquire it in the old profit sharing ratio and so share the future profits in their old ratio.

*For example, Asha, Deepti and Nisha are partners in a firm sharing profits and losses in the ratio of **3:2:1.** If Deepti retires, the new profit sharing ratio between Asha and Nisha will be **3:1,** unless they decide otherwise.*

➢ *The continuing partners may acquire the share in the profits of the retiring/deceased partner in a proportion other than their old ratio, In that case, there is need to compute the new profitsharing ratio among them,and it will be equal to sum total of their respective old share and the share acquired from the retiring/deceased partner.*

New share of Continuing Partner = Old Share + Acquired
share from the Outgoing Partner

1) Gaining share of Continuing Partner = New share – Old share

2) Goodwill Revaluation Method :

ii. *When Goodwill Account is not there in the books of Partnership firm :*

- *For creating Goodwill Account*
  Goodwill A/c   Dr. (Total value of Goodwill)
          To Old Partners Capital A/c   (Old Ratio)

- *For write off Goodwill Account*
          All Partners Capital A/c Dr
          (Excluding Retire Partner)
          To Goodwill A/c (New Ratio)
          (Total value of Goodwill)

iii. *When Goodwill Account is there in the books of Partnership firm :*

- ♣ *When new value of goodwill determined is similar to disclosed value of goodwill.*
- *No entry*

♣ *When New Value of Goodwill is Determined More than the Disclosed Value of Goodwill :*

• *When new value of Goodwill is determined more than the disclosed value of Goodwill at the time of partner Z is retired : (In Old Ratio and Difference between new value of Goodwill and Old value of Goodwill)*

Date	Particulars	Debit Rs.	Credit Rs.
1/4/2012	*Goodwill A/c Dr.* * To X's capital a/c* * To Y's capital a/c* * To Z's capital a/c*		

♣ *When new Value of Goodwill is determined less than disclosed value of Goodwill :*

  • *When new value of Goodwill is determined less than the disclosed value of Goodwill at the time of partner Z is retired: (In Old Ratio and Difference between old value of Goodwill and new value of Goodwill)*

Date	Particulars		Debit Rs.	Credit Rs.
1/4/2012	X's capital a/c	Dr.		
	Y's capital a/c	Dr.		
	To Goodwill a/c			

Note : When Goodwill A/c will be written off at that time Partners Capital A/c (Excluding Retire Partner)will be debited and Goodwill A/c will be credited. (In New Ratio)

☐ THEORY SECTION ☐

❖ ***The Circumstances of a Partner's Retirement :***

1) ***As per the Indian Partnership Act :*** *According to Partnership Act, any partner can be retire under the following circumstances.*

    a) By Consent of all : *Any partner can be retire with the consent of all partners from the partnership firm.*

    b) By Providing Notice : *Partner can be retire from the partnership firm by providing a written notice to other partners of the firm, mentioning intention of retirement.*

    c) By Death of a partner : *A partner automatically ceases to be a partner in the firm by his/her death.*

d) By Expulsion : *Other partner can expel the concerned partner only when there is a provision in the partnership agreement and on fulfillment of the requirements of such provision.*

e) Due to Insolvency : *when any partner of the firm is declared insolvent, he ceases to be a partner and retires compulsorily.*

f) As per the terms of Partnership Agreement/Deed : *A partner can be retire on the basis of terms and conditions of partnership Agreement/ deed.*

2) Voluntary Retirement Due to personal Reason of a Partner : *Any partner due to personal reasons like age factor, illness etc. can take decision to retire himself from the firm.*

It is necessary for an active partner of the firm to issue public notice about his own retirement. Otherwise he is responsible towards third parties for the firm's actions taking place even after his/ her retirement.

⇒ **Memorandum Revaluation Account or Memorandum Profit and Loss Adjustment Account :**

If the partners decide not to show changes arising in the value of assets and liabilities due to revaluation on retirement or death of a partner, then in this situation to incorporate the arising accounting treatment, Memorandum Revaluation Account or Memorandum Profit and Loss Adjustment Account is prepared. This account is to be prepared in following two steps :

*   **Step 1 :** *changes made in the value of assets and liabilities are recorded and arising profit or loss is transferred to partners (including retiring partner) capital accounts.*

*   **Step 2 :** *All given accounting treatment in **step 1** will be brought back (reversed) opposite side at the revaluation account. Arising profit or loss will be transferred to respective sides of partners (remaining) capital account. Since all accounting treatment are revered back from **step 1** to **step 2**, value of assets and liabilities remains unaffected after revaluation.*

> ### Annuity Suspense Account :

Instead of paying immediately the dies of retiring partner, if the dues are paid annually to partner or his inheritors for a specified period of time, it is called annuity. As per this method partner's capital account is closed and balance is transferred to annuity suspense account. The interest is added at a fixed rate on outstanding balance of annuity suspense account and paid amount is debited to annuity suspense account.

If a retired partner or his inheritors dies at any time afterwards, as per the agreement the remaining amount in annuity suspense account is treated as a profit for the firm

and is credited to existing partners' capital accounts. But, when the balance in
annuity suspense account is utilized fully and the retiring partner is alive, he continues to receive the annuity as per the agreement, this payment is treated as loss of the firm. Ti will be debited in profit and loss account.

☐ PRACTICAL SECTION ☐

1) *Madhu, Neha and Tina are partners sharing profits in the ratio of 5:3:2. Calculate new profit sharing ratio and gaining ratio if*

        1. *Madhu retires*
        2. *Neha retires*
        3. *Tina retires.*

2) *Alka, Harpreet and Shreya are partners sharing profits in the ratio of 3:2:1. Alka retires and hershare is taken up by Harpreet and Shreya in the ratio of 3:2. Calculatethe new profit sharing ratio.*

3) *Puja, Priya, Pratistha are partners sharing profits and losses in the ratio of 5 : 3 : 2. Priya retires. Her share is taken by Priya and Pratistha in the ratio of 2 : 1. Calculate the new profit sharing ratio.*

4) Kumar, Lakshya, Manoj and Naresh are partners sharing profits in the ratio of *3 : 2 : 1 : 4*. Kumar retires and his share is acquired by Lakshya and Manoj inthe ratio of *3:2.* Calculate new profit sharing ratio and gaining ratio of the remaining partners.

5) Murli, Naveen and Omprakash are partners sharing profits and loss in the ratio of *1:2:3.* When Omprakash retired, following journal entry was passed for the goodwill.

Murli's capital a/c	Dr.	**2,400**
Naveen's capital a/c	Dr.	**1,200**
To Omprakash's capital a/c		**3,600**

Calculate new profit sharing ratio.

6) The Balance Sheet of Ashish, Suresh and Lokesh who were sharing profits inthe ratio of *5 : 3 : 2,* is given below as on March *31, 2007.*Balance Sheet as on March *31, 2007*

Liabilities	Rs.	Assets	Rs.
Capital :		Land	4,00,000
Ashish : 7,20,000		building	3,80,000
Suresh : 4,15,000		Plant	4,65,000
Lokesh : 3,45,000	14,80,000	Furniture	77,000
General reserve	1,80,000	Stock	1,75,000
Creditors	1,24,000	Debtors	1,72,000
Outstanding Exp.	16,000	Cash	1,21,000
	18,00,000		18,00,000

Suresh retires on the above date and the following

adjustments are agreed upon his retirement.

1. *Stock was valued at* **Rs.1,72,000.**
2. *Furniture were valued at* **Rs.80,000.**
3. *An amount of* **Rs.10,000** *due from Mr.Deepak a debtor, was doubtful and a provision for the same was required.*
4. *Goodwill of the firm was valued at* **Rs.2,00,000** *but it was decided not to show goodwill in the books of accounts.*
5. *Suresh was paid* **Rs.40,000** *immediately on retirement and the balance was transferred to his loan account.*
6. *Ashish and Lokesh were to share future profits in the ratio of* **3:2.**

Prepare Revaluation Account, Capital Account and Balance Sheet of the reconstituted firm.

7) *The Balance Sheet of Mohit, Neeraj and Sohan who are partners in a firm sharing profits according to their capitals as on March* **31, 2009** *was as under:*

Balance sheet

Liabilities	Rs.	Assets	Rs.
Capital Account:		Land-building	1,00,000
Mohit : 80,000		Machinery	50,000
Neeraj : 40,000		Stock	18,000
Sohan : 40,000	1,60,000	Debtors 20,000	
Creditors	21,000	-BDR 1,000	19,000
General reserve	20,000	Cash	14,000
	2,01,000		2,01,000

On that date, Sohan decided to retire from the firm and

was paid for his share in the firm subject to the following:

⇒Buildings to be appreciated by **20%.**

⇒Provision for Bad debts to be increased to **15%** on Debtors.

⇒Machinery to be depreciated by **20%.**

⇒Goodwill of the firm is valued at **Rs.72,000** and the retiring partner's share is adjusted through the capital accounts of remaining partners.

⇒The capital of the new firm be fixed at **Rs.1,20,000** in the new profit sharing ratio.

Prepare Revaluation Account, Capital Accounts of the partners, and the Balance Sheet after retirement of Sohan.

8) Diwali ,Dasera and Holi are partners sharing the profit and loss in equal proportion. The balance sheet of their firm as at **31-12-2011** is as under :

Balance sheet

Liabilities	Amount Rs.	Asset	Amount Rs.
Capital :		Goodwill	2,700
Diwali : **4,500**		Land-building	6,000
Dasera : **3,000**		Investment	7,50
Holi : **3,000**	10,500	Stock	1,500
Profit and loss A/c	600	Debtors	1,380
Creditors	180	Cash	750
Investment fluctuation fund	1,800		
	13,080		13,080

*Holi has retired on **31-12-2011** To meet the payment of the dues of the retiring partner the following is decided.*

- ❖ *The goodwill of the firm is to be valued at an average profit of the last **5** years.*
- ❖ *The value of land building is **Rs. 7,500.***
- ❖ *Maintain investment fluctuation fund of **Rs. 75.***
- ❖ *All debtors are solvent, no BDR is required,*
- ❖ *The value of stock is **Rs. 1,410.***
- ❖ *Figures for the profit of the last **5** years are as follows :*

Years	2007	2008	2009	2010	2011
Profit (Rs.)	1,500	1,200	1,350	2,100	1,725

Write necessary journal entries and prepare the partner's capital account and the new (revised) balance sheet.

9) *Pound , Dollar and Euro are partners of a partnership firm sharing profit in the **4:3:2**.. The balance sheet of their firm as on **31-12-10** as under :*

Balance sheet as on **31-12-10**

Liabilities	Amount Rs.	Assets	Amount Rs.
Capital :		Land & Building	25,000
Pound : 15,000		Machinery	10,000
Dollar : 10,000		Investments	5,000
Euro : 5,000	30,000	Stock	5,000

General reserve	3,000	Debtors	10,000	
Creditors	22,000	−BDR	1,000	9,000
		Cash balance		1,000
	18,800			18,800

Euro has given a notice for separation from the partnership firm. They have agreed upon the following terms are decided.

i.   The value of the Land and Building is to be increased by **20%**.

ii. Depreciate machinery at **10%**.

iii. The market value of the Investments is **20%** more than the book value.

iv. Provide **5% BDR**.

v.   Firm's goodwill is determined at **Rs.15,000.** For the share of Euro's goodwill entry is to be given to Pound and Dollar's capital accounts.

vi. Outstanding **Rs.1,000** towards the salary of an employee.

vii. **Rs.12,000** is the estimated profit till the retirement date of Euro.

viii. Pound and Dollar have to bring cash for all the dues to Euro and to maintain cash balance of **Rs.7,000** as the working capital and the new capital of the new firm should be in their profit sharing ratio.

From the above information prepare necessary accounts and Balance Sheet in the books of the firm.

⌐ LATEST EXAMINATION ⌐

10) *Raghav and Madhav are partners of a partnership firm sharing profit in the ratio 7:3. The balance sheet of their partnership firm as on 31-12-07 is as under.*

Balance sheet as on 31-12-07

Liabilities	Amount Rs.	Assets	Amount Rs.
Capital :		Land & Building	10,000
Raghav : 20,000		Machinery	10,000
Madhav : 10,000	30,000	Stock	10,000
General reserve	10,000	Debtors	10,000
Creditors	12,000	Motorcar	10,000
		Cash balance	2,000
	52,000		52,000

Madhav retires on 1-01-2008. Revaluation of assets is fixed as follows :

Land & Building Rs.20,000, Machinery Rs.15,000, Stock Rs.5,000, written off Rs.2,000 from debtors, stationary bill of Rs.300 is outstanding for payment, which is recorded in the books.

Madhav would take over the motor car in such a way that his due amount would retain in firm as a loan at 10 % to earn an interest of Rs.1,000 per annum.

Prepare necessary accounts and also prepare the Balance sheet after retirement of Madhav

(March,09)

11) Saturday, Sunday and Monday are partners of a partnership firm sharing profit in the **4:3:2..** The balance sheet of their firm as on **31-12-10** as under :

Balance sheet as on **31-12-10**

Liabilities	Rs.	Assets	Rs.
Capital :		Land & Building	9,000
Saturday : 7,200		Plant & Machinery	3,060
Sunday : 5,400		Stock	2,800
Monday : 3,600	16,200	Debtors 1,800	
Creditors	2,400	–BDR 60	1,740
Expenses liability	200	Cash balance	2,200
	18,800		18,800

Monday has given a notice for separation from the partnership firm. They have agreed upon the following terms are decided.

ix. The value of the Land and Building is to be increased by **20%**.

x. The value of the stock is to be increased by **Rs.280**.

xi. Now BDR is not required.

xii. Firm's goodwill is determined at **Rs.1,800** to be shown in the books.

xiii. *Rs.20 outstanding for receivable interest.*

xiv. *From the dues of Monday, **Rs.2,000** are to be retained in the firm as loan and the remaining amount is to be paid in cash. The working capital of the firm is determined at **Rs.2,000.***

xv. *The continuing partners have decided to maintain their capital in their new profit sharing rating proportion **3:2** for which either they would bring or withdrew cash.*

From the above information prepare necessary accounts and Balance Sheet in the books of the firm.

(March,10)

12) *Morli, Bansi and Vasu are partners in equal proportion. The balance sheet of their firm as on **31-12-08** as under :*

*Balance sheet as on **31-12-08***

Liabilities		Rs.	Assets		Rs.
Capital :			Goodwill		10,000
Morli :	20,000		Land & Building		25,000
Bansi :	15,000		Machinery		15,000
Vasu :	10,000	45,000	Investments		5,000
General reserve		4,500	Stock		5,000
Bank overdraft		5,000	Debtors	5,000	
Creditors		20,000	–BDR	500	4,500
Provident fund		7,500	Cash balance		17,500
		82,000			82,000

*Vasu retired on **1-01-09**. On the same day, the following terms are decided.*

a) Fixed assets to be appreciated by 20%.

b) Reduce stock value by 10%.

c) Out of creditors Rs.1,000 are not payable.

d) Bank overdraft interest is 10%. Interest of last year is yet to be recorded.

e) Goodwill of the firm has been revalued but it is decided that the goodwill has to be shown in the books as per its old value.

f) Accrued Income of commission is Rs.1,000 , which is to be recorded in the books.

g) Rs.16,500 paid in cash to Vasu towards his dues.

Prepare the necessary accounts to incorporate the above transaction and also prepare balance sheet after retirement of Vasu.   **(March,11)**

13) *Amar, Akbar and Anthony are partners in equal proportion. The balance sheet of their firm as on **31-03-09** is as under :*

Balance sheet as on 31-03-09

Liabilities	Rs.	Asset	Rs.
Capital Account		Plant	2,70,000
Amar : 1,80,000		Building	1,80,000
Akbar : 2,70,000		Stock	90,000
Anthony : 1,80,000	6,30,000	Debtors	90,000
Sundry Creditors	90,000	Cash / Bank	90,000
	7,20,000		7,20,000

*Anthony has decided to take retirement on **31-03-09** and the remaining partners have continued the business. On the same day assets and liabilities are revalued as follows.*

1) *Provide **10%** depreciation on Plant.*
2) *Increase the value of building by **20%**.*
3) *Closing sock is valued at **Rs.75,000**.*
4) *Provide **10%** for bad debts reserve.*
5) *Income which is accrued not received and recorded in the books is **Rs.15,000**.*
6) *Firm's goodwill is determined at **Rs.2,10,000**. Anthony's share of goodwill is directly recorded to the capital account of Amar and Akbar.*
7) *The total capital of the new firm would remain as it was before retirement of Anthony, and this will be in the new profit sharing ratio. The new profit sharing ratio is **1:1**.*
8) *All dues of Anthony are to be paid in cash.*

Prepare the necessary accounts to incorporate the above transaction and also prepare balance sheet after retirement of Anthony. **(March,12) (March,14- 1/3 amount)**

14) *Kanu, Manu and Jashu are partners sharing the profit in the ratio **1: 2 :2**.*

Balance Sheet as on 31-3-2009

Liabilities		Rs.	Assets	Rs.
Capital			Building	40,000
Kanu	30,000		Machinery	30,000
Manu	20,000		Stock	10,000
Jashu	10,000	60,000	Debtors	10,000

Creditors	40,000	Cash	20,000
Workmen accident	10,000	P & L a/c	10,000
Comp. fund		Bills receivable	30,000
Provident fund	10,000		
Bills payable	30,000		
	1,50,000		1,50,000

Jashu retires from the partnership from on **31-3-09** assets and liabilities are revalued as follows.

Machinery **Rs.25,000** ,building **Rs.50,000**, stock **Rs. 12,000** and debtors of **Rs.2,000** found to be doubtful.

From the above information prepare the necessary accounts and also the new balance sheet. **(March,13)**

............xxxxxxxxx............

CHAPTER – 3

("DISSOLUTION OF PARTNERSHIP FIRM")

🗋 THEORY SECTION 🗋

❖ **Dissolution of Partnership**

" From the existing partners of the firm, if any of the partner or partners retire or expires or declared insolvent. In such a case, partnership gets dissolved then it is known as dissolution of partnership. "

As stated earlier dissolution of partnership changes the existing relationship between partners but the firm may continue its business as before. The dissolution of partnership may take place in any of the following ways:

(1) Change in existing profit sharing ratio among partners;

(2) Admission of a new partner;

(3) Retirement of a partner;

(4) Death of a partner;

(5) Insolvency of a partner;

(6) Completion of the venture, if partnership is formed for that; and

(7) Expiry of the period of partnership, if partnership is for a specific period of time;

❖ **Dissolution of a firm**

"When all the activities of the partnership firm are closed and firm losses its legal existence forever then it is known as dissolution of partnership firm."

Dissolution of a partnership firm may take place without the intervention of court or by the order of a court, in any of the ways specified later in this section.It may be noted that dissolution of the firm necessarily brings in dissolution of the partnership.

Dissolution of a firm takes place in any of the following ways:

*1) **Dissolution by Agreement:** A firm is dissolved :*

    (a) with the consent of all the partners or

    (b) in accordance with a contract between the partners.

*2)**Compulsory Dissolution:** A firm is dissolved compulsorily in the following cases*

 (a) when all the partners or all but one partner, become insolvent, rendering them incompetent to sign a contract;

(b) when the business of the firm becomes illegal; or

(c) when some event has taken place which makes it unlawful for the partners to carry on thebusiness of the firm in partnership e.g.when a partnerwho is a citizen of a country becomes an alien enemy because of the declaration of war with hiscountry and India.

*3)**On the happening of certain contingencies:** Subject to contract between the partners, a firm is dissolved :*

    a) if constituted for a fixed term, by the expiry of that term;

    b) if constituted to carry out one or more ventures, by the completion thereof;

c) by the death of a partner;

d) by the adjudication of a partner as an insolvent.

4) **Dissolution by Notice:** *In case of partnership at will, the firm may be dissolved if any one of the partners gives a notice in writing to the other partners,signifying his intention of seeking dissolution of the firm.*

5) **Dissolution by Court:** *At the suit of a partner, the court may order a partnership firm to be dissolved on any of the following grounds:* **(March ,10)**

   a) *when a partner becomes insane;*

   b) *when a partner becomes permanently incapable of performing his duties as a partner;*

   c) *when a partner is guilty of misconduct which is likely to adversely affect the business of the firm;*

   d) *when a partner persistently commits breach of partnership agreement;*

   e) *when a partner has transferred the whole of his interest in the firm to a third party;*

   f) *when the business of the firm cannot be carried on except at a loss; or*

   g) *when, on any ground, the court regards dissolution to be just and equitable.*

➢ *Realization Account* **(March ,09)**

Specimen of Realization Account

Particulars	(Rs)	Particulars	(Rs)
To Assets Accounts :		By Liabilities Accounts :	
To Land and Building	✓	By Sundry creditors	✓
To Plant and Machinery	✓	By Bills payable	✓
To Furniture and Fittings	✓	By Bank overdraft	✓
To Bills receivable	✓	By Outstanding expenses	✓
To Sundry debtors	✓	By Provision for doubtful debts	✓
To Cash / Bank Account (Payment of liabilities) (Payment of unrecorded liabilities)	✓	By Cash / Bank Account : (sale of assets)	✓
		By Partner's capital account : (assets taken by partner)	✓
To Partner's capital account : (Liability assumed by partner)	✓		
To Profit : (Transferred to partners capital account in their profit sharing ratio)	✓	By Loss : (Transferred to partners capital account in their profit sharing ratio)	✓
	✓		✓

When the firm is dissolved, its books of account are to be closed and the profit orloss arising on realisation of its assets and discharge of liabilities is to be computed. For this purpose a Realisation Account is prepared to ascertain the net effect (profit or loss) of realisation of assets and payment of liabilities Which may be is transferred to partner's capital accounts in their profit sharing ratio. Hence, all assets (other than cash in hand bank balance and fictitious assets, if any),and all external liabilities are transferred to this account.It also records the sale of assets, and payment of liabilities and realisation expenses. The balance in this account is termed as profit or loss on realisation which is transferred to partners' capital accounts in thier profit sharing ratio.

❋ ***Normal Procedure for dissolution of firm :***

*1) **Realization Account :** The account prepared to pass necessary accounting treatment for the disposal of assets and payment of liabilities of the firm is known as Realization Account. On dissolution of the firm the assets accounts (Except cash and bank) and liabilities accounts are closed and transferred to Realization A/c at their book value. The realized value on sale of asset is recorded on credit side of Realization Account and the amount paid for the liability is debited to Realization Account. Dissolution expenses are also debited to Realization Account.*

The balancein this account is termed as profit or loss on realisation which is transferred to partners' capital accounts in thier profit sharing ratio.

2) **Partner's Loan Account :** *If any partners have advanced a loan to the firm, then separately partner's loan account is prepared. Such loan account has a credit balance and on payment of such loan, the loan account will be debited and that account is closed.*

3) **Partner's Capital/ Current Account :** *After closing the loan account, the balance of the current account is transferred to the respective partner's capital account. Now all partners are paid with the balnce amount in their capital accounts. If a debit balance is there in partner's capital account, then that partner has to bring the amount of such debit balance in cash. Thus, the capiatl account will be closed.*

4) **Cash / Bank Account :** *Cash / Bank Account is squared up i.e. it becomes equal from both sides as soon as partners capital accounts are settled and closed.*

⇒**Four accounts are to be opened to close books of accounts, when partnership firm is dissolved : (March ,10)**
   1. *Realization Account*
   2. *Partner's Loan Account*
   3. *Partner's Capital/ Current Account*
   4. *Cash / Bank Account*

⇒   **Accounting Treatment :**

1.   **For tranasfer of assets :**
   All asset accounts excluding cash, bank and the fictitious assets, if any areclosed by transfer to the debit of Realisation Account at their book values. It may be noted

that sundry debtors are transferred at gross value and the provision for doubtful debts is transferred to the credit side of Realisation Account along with liabilities. The same thing will apply to fixed assets, if provision for depreciation account is maintained.

Realisation A/c   Dr.

To Assets (Individually) A/c

2.   **For transfer of liabilities :**

All external liability accounts including provisions, if an are closed by transferring them to the credit of Realisation account.

Liabilities (individually) Dr.

To Realisation A/c

3.   **For sale of assets :**

Bank A/c Dr.

To Realisation A/c

4.   **For an asset taken over by a partner :**

Partner's Capital A/c Dr.

To Realisation A/c

5.   **For payment of liabilities :**

Realisation A/c   Dr.

To Bank A/c

6.   **For a liability which a partner takes responsibility to discharge :**

Ralisation A/cDr.

To Partner's Capital A/c

7. *For settlement with the creditor through transfer of assets when a creditor accepts an asset in full and final settlement of his account, journal entry needs to be recorded. But, if the creditor accepts an asset only as part payment of his/her dues, the entry will be made for cash payment only. For example,a creditor to whom* **Rs.10,000** *was due accepts office equipment worth* **Rs.8,000** *and is paid* **Rs.2,000** *in cash, the following entry s hall be made for the payment of* **Rs.2,000** *only.*

> *Realisation A/c   Dr.*
> *   To Bank A/c*

However, when a creditor accepts an asset whose value is more than the amount due to him, he/she will pay cash to the frim for the difference for which the entry will be:

> *Bank A/c Dr.*
> *   To Realisation A/c*

8. **Realisation of any unrecorded assets including goodwill, if any**

> *Bank A/c Dr.*
> *   To Realisation A/c*

9. **For settlement of any unrecorded liability :**

> *Realisation A/c   Dr.*
> *To Bank A/c*

10. **For transfer of profit and loss on realisation :**

(a) In case of profit on realisation

> *Realisation A/c   Dr.*

To Partners' Capital A/c (individually) A/c

(b) In case of loss on realisation

Partners' Capital A/c (individually)   Dr.

To Realisation A/c

11. For transfer of accumulated profits in the form of reserve fund or general reserve:

Reserve Fund/General Reserve A/c   Dr.

To Partners' Capital A/c (individually)

12. For transfer of fictitious assets, if any, to partners' capital accounts in their profit sharing ratio:

Partners' Capital A/c (individually) Dr.

To Fictitious Asset A/c

13. For payment of loans due to partners :

Partner's Loan A/c Dr.

To Bank A/c

14. For settlement of partners' accounts :

If the partner's capital account shows a debit balance, he brings in the necessary cash for which the entry will be:

Bank A/c Dr.

To Partner's Capital A/c

The balance is paid to partners whose capital accounts show a credit balance and the following entry is recorded.

Partners' Capitals A/cs (individually) Dr.

To Bank A/c

It may be noted that the aggregate amount finally payable to the partners must equal to he amount available in bank and cash accounts.Thus,all accounts of a firm are closed in case of dissolution.

✱ Difference Between First Method and Second Method. (March 10,12)

No.	Points	First Method	Second Method
1.	**Realization A/c**	*After closing assets and liabilities accounts they are transferred to Realization A/c.*	*Assets and liabilities accounts are not transferred to Realization A/c.*
2.	**Accounts**	*Assets and liabilities accounts they are closed.*	*Assets and liabilities accounts they are not closed. After realizing assets and payment of liabilities theses accounts are closed.*
3.	**Realization of Assets**	*The realized value on sale of asset is recorded on credit side of Realization Account.*	*The realized value of the asset is credited to asset account and the balance is transferred to Realization Account.*
4.	**Payment of liability**	*The amount paid for the liability is debited to Realization Account.*	*The amount paid for the liability is debited to that liability account and the balance is transferred to Realization Account.*
5.	**Circumstances**	*If the assets are realized*	*If the realization of asset and payment of liability are made*

		immediately and liabilities are paid instantly on dissolution then this method is suitable.	in installments on dissolution, then this method is suitable.

❒ PRACTICAL SECTION ❒

1. How would you deal with the following items of balance sheet in case of dissolution of a partnership firm :
   - ❖ Investment Fluctuation Fund
   - ❖ Depreciation Fund
   - ❖ Provident Fund
   - ❖ Debit Balance of P & L Account

2. State whether the following statements are true or False. Correct the False statement with proper of firm.
   1) When a single (one) partner of a firm retires, the firm gets dissolved.
   2) The court can interfere with regard to any matter of dissolution of a partnership firm.
   3) To pay the liabilities of a partnership firm, the personal assets of partner can't be used.
   4) The loan of partner's wife from the woman's personal wealth of possession is paid prior to any payment towards the third party liability.
   5) In partnership firm, the liabilities of all partners are confined to their capital only.

6) *Workmen profit sharing fund is distributed amongst partners in their profit and loss sharing ratio.*

7) *At the time of dissolution of a partnership firm unrecorded contingent liability is debited to the realization account and credited to that liability account.*

8) *The status of debtors at the time of dissolution was as follows :*

Balance sheet

Liabilities	Amount	Assets	Amount
		Debtors **2,00,000**	
		-BDR **20,000**	**1,80,000**

*During dissolution the accounting treatment of debtors will be given at the debit side of realization account by **Rs.1,80,000.***

9) *The dissolution expenses of the firm is to be paid by the firm itself, But if it is paid by any partner, no accounting treatment is required in the books.*

10) *Bad debts recovery is not required to be recorded in the books.*

3. **Write accounting treatments for the following transaction in case (in event) of dissolution of a firm :**

A. *Goodwill is not shown in the books. But during dissolution **Rs.30,000** are realized on sale of it.*

B. *Rs.2,00,000 for land building and Rs.1,50,000 for investments are disclosed in the balance sheet for which Rs.1,80,000 and Rs.1,80,000 are realized respectively.*

C. *Write journal entry for the remaining surplus of assets of Rs.1,20,000 which is available after making payment towards all liabilities and payment of partners loan. (**The Profit sharing ratio of partners is 5:3:2)***

D. *A partner has accepted responsibility for dissolution process and the firm has decided to pay remuneration in exchange of his service of Rs.20,000 The firm has paid Rs.10,000 remuneration to him.*

E. *A Partner has accepted to pay the loan of his wife (loan given to firm) of Rs.15,000.*

F. *Taxation liability is paid of at Rs.5,500 which is not recorded in the books.*

G. *The following treatment is given investments at the time of dissolution in the books of X ltd.*

Profit and loss Account of Assets Realization

Particulars	Amount	Particulars	Amount
To Investment a/c (book value)	1,50,000	By Cash a/c (realization)	1,80,000
	1,50,000		1,80,000

State whether the above mentioned accounting treatment is correct or not. If it is incorrect correct it and rewrite the journal entry.

H. At the time of dissolution, goodwill is disclosed in the books at **Rs.80,000** no informal is available about its realizable value.

I. At the time of dissolution motor car is disclosed in the books at **Rs.75,000** this is taken over by one partner for **Rs.25,000.**

J. At the time of dissolution , furniture is disclosed in the books at **Rs.17,000** no information is available about its realizable value.

☐ LATEST EXAMINATION ☐

4. How would you deal with the following items of balance sheet in case of dissolution of a partnership firm ?
i.   Depreciation fund
ii. Credit balance of profit and loss account

OR

Write accounting treatment for the following transaction in case of dissolution of a firm.

i. Goodwill is not shown in the books, but during dissolution **Rs.10,000** are realized on sale on it.

ii. Taxation liability is determined at **Rs.20,000** ,which is not recorded in the books. (**March 09**)

5. Write accounting treatment for the following transaction in case of dissolution of a firm.

1. *At the time of dissolution , goodwill is disclosed in the books at* **Rs.30,000.** *No information is available about its realize value.*

2. *At the time of dissolution, Motor car is disclosed in the books at* **Rs.1,00,000.** *One partner namely " M " has taken over this motor car at* **Rs.60,000.**

3. *At the time of dissolution, furniture is disclosed in the books at* **Rs.20,000** *. No information is available about its realize value.* **(March 09)**

6. *State whether the following statements are true or false. Correct the false statement with proper explanation.*

  * *Workmen profit sharing fund is distributed amongst partners in their profit and loss sharing ratio.*

  * *When a single partner of a firm retires, the firm get dissolved.*

  * *In partnership firm, the liabilities of all partners are confined to their capital only.*

  * *Workmen compensation fund / Labour accident relief fund is distributed amongst partners in their profit and loss sharing ratio.***(March,12)**

  * *At the time of dissolution of a partnership firm unrecorded contingent liability is debited to the realization account and credited to that liability account.***(March 10,12)**

7. *State whether the following statements are true or false. Correct the false statement with proper explanation.*

⇒ *The court can interfere with regard to any matter of dissolution of a partnership firm.*

⇒ *Bad debts recovery is not required to be recorded in the books.* **(March 11, 12)**

8. *Total assets of X and Y's firm are **Rs.1,50,000**. In which cash is of **Rs.10,000** . Net assets of the firm are **Rs.1,00,000**. The ratio of the capital and reserve is **4:1**. The capital of X is more than the capital of Y by **Rs.20,000**. The firm is dissolved. The loss of realization account is **Rs.20,000**. Prepare the dissolution accounts for the firm.*

(March 11)

9. *Write accounting treatment for the following transaction in case of dissolution of a firm.*

1. *At the time of dissolution , goodwill is disclosed in the books at **Rs.28,000**. No information is available about its realize value.*

2. *At the time of dissolution, Motor car is disclosed in the books at **Rs.60,000**. One partner namely "Yash" has taken over this motor car at **Rs.45,000**.*

3. *At the time of dissolution, furniture is disclosed in the books at **Rs.18,000**. No information is available about its realize value.* **(March 11)**

10. *Pass the journal entry of following transactions in which in the case of dissolution of partnership firm.*

➢ Receipt **Rs.10,000** of goodwill, which is not mentioned in the book at the time of dissolution of partnership firm.

➢ Partner Ashok accepts to pay the bills payable of **Rs.20,000.(March 12)**

11. Pass the journal entry for the following cases while the realization account is made by second method.

✗ The book value of Machinery is **Rs. 45,000,** is taken by partner Ankit at **Rs.47,500.**

✗ Partner Bimal accepts to pay the bills payable of **Rs.9,000.**

✗ **Rs.7,000** is received from bad debts return for **Rs.9,000.**

(March 12)

12. How would you deal with the following items of balance sheet in case of dissolution of partnership firm ?
(i) Credit balance of profit & loss a/c
(ii) Investment Fluctuation fund

OR

A partner has accepted responsibility for dissolution process and the firm has decided to pay remuneration in exchange of his service Of **Rs.10,000** The firm has paid. **Rs.5,000** as expenses to him. Write down journal entry. **(March 12,13)**

13. Explain in brief legal provision with regards to dissolution of firm (Any three)   **(March 13,14)**

14. State whether the following statement are true or false. Correct the false statement.

(i) In the event of dissolution, goodwill shown in the balance sheet is transferred to capital A/c in profit & loss ratio.

(ii) If all partners becomes insolvent or business becomes illegal then firm will be dissolve.

(iii) In partnership firm, if one partner gets retired then firm gets dissolved. **(March 13)**

15. At the time of dissolution debtors were valued at **Rs.80,000** and creditor's were valued at **Rs.40,000.** Creditors are paid at **20 %** discount by one partner. Write down 'Journal Entry' to close the books of the firm. **(March '14)**

16. State whether the following statements are true or false. Correct the false statements and rewrite them.

1) To pay dissolution expenses is responsibility of the firm.

2) When no information is available for realization of tangible assets, then it will be taken as zero.

3) At the time of dissolution debts will be paid at book value.

(March 14)

17. At the time of dissolution, furniture of **Rs.20,000** was written in the books. No information is available about **its** realizable value. Write down ' journal entry' to close the books of the firm. **(March 14)**

...........××××××××××...........

Chapter-4

"Accounting for Debenture"

☐ THEORY SECTION ☐

♣ **Meaning of debenture and types of debentures.**

Meaning : *Sometimes company borrows long term funds from the public. Against the money so borrowed the company issues a document acknowledgment its debt to the investor. Such a document is known as a debenture.*

Explanation : *debenture4 is a document that confirms the debt of the company and its acknowledgment of the debt. It is issued under the common seal of the company.*

1) Based on security :

Secured of mortgage debentures : *when this type of debentures are issued by the company some or all of the assets of the company are given as security such a charge could be of two crated on the assets of the company such a charge could be of two types : fixed charge or floating charge the company can't dispose of such charged or mortgaged assets without the consent of the debenture holders.*

2) Simple or unsecured or naked debenture : *when the company issues the debentures without giving any security or creating any charge on the assets of the company. Then such debenture are known as simple or unsecured or naked debentures on such debentures, the company only gives a promise to pay the interest on debenture the company only gives a promise to pay the interest on the due dates and the repayment of the principal amount on the date of maturity such debentures are risky for the investor.*

3) Based on conditions of redemption :

1) redemption debenture : *the debentures which are issued with a condition that the amount of debentures can be repaid after a certain period are known as redeemable debentures the period of redemption is stated by the company in the debenture or trust deed.*

2) Irredeemable debentures : *when nothing is mentioned about the specific time at which the amount of debenture will be repaid are known as irredeemable debentures generally, money borrowed against such debentures is repaid at the time of liquidation of the company.*

3) Based on negotiability and record viewpoint :

1) Registered debentures : *for the transfer of such debentures it is essential to get the transfer registered with the company and the company makes an entry of the transfer in register* *maintained by it. The register contains the name, address and other particulars related to debenture holders.*

2) Bearer debentures : *there is no need to register the transfer of such debentures with the company. Such debentures are like currency notes. The interest commons are attached with such debentures for periodic interest payments :*

3) Based on convertibility :

1) Convertible debenture : *the debentures which can be converted into equity or is automatically converted into shares for full or part of the amount of the debentures after a specified period are known as convertible debentures*

2) Non-Convertible debenture : *The debentures which cannot be converted into equity shares or preference shares are known as Non-Convertible debenture.*

3) Based on priority of redemption :

1) First debentures : *the debentures have first charge on the assets given as security and are repaid before any other debentures are paid off are known as first debenture*

2) Second debentures : *the debentures are paid off only after the first charge of the first debentures are paid off are known as second debentures.*

❖ _Formalities for the issue of debentures and related provisions of the companies act._

The formalities for the issue of debentures and related provisions of the companies act are as under :

1) **_A resolution in board of directors meeting :_** _when it is decided to issue of debentures a resolution is passed in the meeting of board of directors of the company. The resolution should state the amount of the debentures the number of debentures rate of interest thereon and other terms related to the issue of the debentures._

2) **_Prospectus :_** _for the issue of the debentures a company should issue a prospectus inviting the public to subscribe for debentures giving full information as required :_

3) **_Appointment of trustees :_** _if the debentures are redeemable beyond a period of 18 months from the date of issue, debentures trustees are required to be appointed and a debenture redemption fund is also required to be created._

4) **_Credit rating :_** _for public subscription or rights offer to debentures credit rating by a recognized rating agency is also mandatory._

5) **_Bank account in a scheduled bank :_** _when debentures are issued to the public. The money received on the application has to be kept credited in a scheduled bank in a separate account. The company secretary prepares a list of applications received and the company secretary prepares_

a list of applications received and the statement of allotment after the closer of public subscription

6) A resolution for allotment : *the secretary would inform the applicants about the allotment of debentures to them after the directors pass a resolution for allotment of debentures.*

♣ Debentures issued as collateral security

When a company borrows money or avails of an overdraft from the bank. It sometimes given its own debentures as security the debentures so issued are known as debentures issued as collateral security.

Explanations *: if the company repays its dues to the bank, the bank will return the debentures to the company and the debentures so received are cancelled by the company.*

However, if the company fails to repay the dues to the bank by the due date, the bank can recover its money by setting off the debentures in the market.

The persons purchasing the debentures from the bank will get all the of the debenture holders.

Methods :

1) Debentures given to a bank as security are only for the security of the loan.

2) No accounting entry is passed in the books of the company the same. However along with the bank loan the same will be shown in the inner alumni under the heading secured loan on the liability side of the balance sheet.

3) If a company fails to ready the bank loan, the bank becomes the owner of such debentures in such circumstance accounting entry is passed in the books of the company for debentures.

4) If the debentures given as collateral security are to be recorded in the books of account the entry will be as under :

Date	Particulars	L.F	Debit	Credit
	Debenture suspense A/c Dr To.........% debentures a/c (entry for giving debentures of Rs..... as collateral security to the bank against a loan of Rs.....)			

In such circumstances, debentures a/c will be shown on the liability side of the balance sheet and the debenture suspense a/c will be shown on the asset side of the balance sheet. If the money due to the bank is repaid and the above entry in the books of the company will be reversed.

♣ Debentures issued for consideration other than cash.

When the issue of debentures by the company against the purchased of assets like plant and machinery land and *building etc. them it is called debentures issued for consideration other than cash*

Generally, the company pays cash or cheque against the purchase of assets. But sometimes the company issues debentures to vendor of business against purchase of assets.

Date	Particulars	L.F	Debit	Credit
	Sundry assets a/c Dr			
	To sundry liabilities a/c			
	To vendor of business a/c			
	Entry for purchase of business assets and liabilities			
	Vendor of business a/c Dr.			
	To .....% debenture a/c			
	Entry for issue of debentures of the company against purchase price.			

♣ Debenture stock :

For convenience, when debentures are issued as a total amount without any denominations like number of debentures, it is known as debenture stock.

In case of debenture stock no individual debentures with fixed nominal value are issued.

Debenture stock holder can sell any part of debenture stock held by him to others and the same can be transferred in the name of the buyer.

A company issues debenture stock certificate to the holders of debenture stock for the value of the stock held by them debentures with face value can be converted into debenture stock.

Generally, debenture stock is secured through trust deed executed for the debenture stock. In exceptional cases, such stock is unsecured.

♣ ***Zero interest debentures :***

The company is not paying any interest o such debentures however, the public is invited to subscribe to such debentures at a high rate of discount and such debentures are redeemed at a nominal value on the due date. The difference between the two amounts the redemption value and issue price is a reward or gain for the investors, which they receive in lieu of interest.

- such gain for the investors us taxable.

- debentures interest is not payable every year by the company.

- is does not have any effect on the cash flow working capital of the company.

♣ *Difference between Debenture premium and premium on redemption of debentures.*

No.	Debenture premium	Premium on redemption of debentures.
1	Debenture premium is a capital debenture Profit for the company	Premium on redemption of is a liability for the company.
2	A company get debenture premium payable at the time of issue of debtors	Such a premium which is by the company to the debenture holders at the time of redemption
3	Amount of debenture premium is to be debenture Utilized for writing off fictitious assets Like share or debenture discount, issue Preliminary.	premium on redemption of debenture is a loss to the company and is therefore debited to loss on issue of debenture a/c and it is written off Gradually every year to profit and loss account.
4	The amount of debenture premium is shown under the heading reserves	The remaining amount of premium on redemption of debentures is shown Under the heading of

And surplus in the balance sheet	'miscellaneous" Expenditure on the asset side of the Balance sheet.

♣ **Difference between Share and debenture.**

Share	Debenture
1. Share is a ownership capital of the company.	Debenture is a borrowed capital of the company.
2. Issue of shares will be compulsory by the company	Issue of debentures will not be composure by the company.
3. Shareholders are received part of the profit dividend of the company.	Debenture holders are received interest as per the terms.
4. There is no surety of the return in the form of dividend on share, irrespective of profit or loss	surety of interest is there as per the terms and conditions of the issue of debenture irrespective of profit or loss.
5. A shareholder is an owner of the company.	A debenture holder is a creditor of the company.
6. No mortgagor charge is created in favour of shareholders when shares are issued.	Generally, a charge is crested on the assets of the company when debentures are issued.
7. Shares cannot be converted into debenture	Debentures which can be converted into shares can be issued.

8. a company is not required to return the share capital during its life time.	Generally, proceeds of debentures are to be repaid after a fixed period.
9. Shares are more risky.	Debentures are very low risky.
10. The shareholders have a right to take part in the administration of the company and have voting right.	Debentures holders do not have voting rights or the right to take part in the administration of the company.
11. Provisions of the companies act have to be complied with to issue shares at discount.	There is no restriction in the companies act on issue of the debentures at discount.
12.in case of liquidation of a company. The shareholders are paid any sum only after paying off all outside liabilities.	In case of liquidation of a company. The debenture holders are paid in priority to the shareholders

♣ **The balance of debenture account, debenture premium account, premium on redemption of debenture account and debenture discount. Or discount on issue of debenture account in the balance sheet of a company.**

➢ **Debenture account** : on the liabilities side of the balances sheet under the head of secured loan.

➤ **Debenture premium account :** on the liabilities side of the balance sheet under the head of reserves and surplus

➤ **Premium on redemption of debenture account :** on the liabilities side of the balance sheet under the head of 'provisions'

➤ **Debenture discount or discount on issue of debenture account :** on the assets and receivables side of the balance sheet under the head of 'miscellaneous expenditure'

📑 **PRACTICAL SECTION** 📑

1. On **1-4-2000** a limited company issued debentures of **Rs.2,50,000** at a discount of **10 %** At the end of every year, a sum of **Rs.50,000** is to be redeemed out of this amount and is to be paid to debenture holders., Prepare a debentures discount account in the books of the company.

2. On **1-1-1999** Sharda Ltd. Issued **20,000 9 %** debentures of **Rs.100** each. According to the terms **of** the debentures, the debentures were to be redeemed at **5%** premium by giving 6 months notice at **any** time after **5** years. The redemption was to be made by cash or by issue of new shares or by issue **of** new debentures as per the option to be exercised by the debenture holders.

   On **1 February 2004** the company issued the required notice to the debenture holders for the redemption of the debentures The company gave three options to the *debentures holders for the redemption of debentures on 1-8-2001 (1) Redemption proceeds will be paid in Cash (2) 10 % Preference shares of Rs.100 each will be issued at Rs.120 per share (3) New 8 % debentures of Rs.100 each will be issued at a price of Rs.96 per debentures.*

Holders of 6000 debentures accepted 10 % Preference Shares holders of 7200 debentures accepted 8 % new debentures and the rest of debentures holders opted for cash payment on redemption.

Write the necessary journal entries to record the above transaction in the books of the company.

3. *Ankleshwar Chemicals Ltd. Issued 4000 7% debentures of Rs.100 each at a price of Rs.95 per debentures The amount payable per debentures was as under.*

   Rs.25 on application (net of Discount)

   Rs.35 on allotment

   Rs.35 on call

   The company received all the money due on allotment. Call money was not received on 300 debentures On all other debentures the amount was received on 300 debentures on all other debentures, the amount was received. Pass the necessary journal entries in the books of the company to record the above transactions.

4. *On 1-4-2011 Meghji Ltd issued 4000 7.5 % debentures of Rs.100 each at 5 % discount. Accounting year of the company ends on 31 st march. Debentures were redeemed at par as under.*

On 31-3-2002   **Rs.1,00,000**

On 31-3- 2003   **Rs.2,00,000**

On 31-3-2004   **Rs.1,00,000**

Pass journal entry in the books of the company for the issue of debentures and prepare a debenture discount account.

5. *On 1-1- 2001 Banwari Ltd. Issued 5000 8 % debentures of* **Rs.100 each at a discount of 6%** *Accounting year of the company ends on* **31 st December** *The debentures were redeemed as under:*

Debentures were redeemed as under :

Date	**Numbers of debentures redeemed**
31-12-2001	2000
31-12-2002	1000
31-12-2003	1600
31-12-2004	400

Prepare a debentures discount account in the books of the company.

6. *On 1-4-2003 Rajvi Ltd. Issued* **20,000, 9 %** *debentures of* **Rs.100** *each at* **10 %** *discount.* **The** *Company is to redeem debentures of* **Rs.5,00,000** *every year. First redemption was started from* **31-3-2004.**

Write all the journal entries relating to debentures in the books of the company for the year ended **31-3-2004.**

8. *Pass the necessary journal entries in the books of the company for the issued and redemption of debentures under the following cases:*

(1) Issued 50,000 debentures of Rs.100 each on 1-1-98 at par, which were redeemed on 1-1-2005 at 20 % premium.

(2) On 1-4-99 issued 80,000debentures of Rs.100 each at 5 % discount, which were redeemed on 31-3-2005 at 10 % premium.

9. *Karnavati Textiles Ltd. Issued 9 % debentures of Rs.100 each on the following terms :*

1. *30,000 debentures at Rs.98*

2. *Issued 8000 debentures of Rs.100 each against purchase of machinery of Rs.10,00,000.*

3. *Issued 9000 debentures of Rs.100 each as collateral security against loan of Rs.5,00,000.*

   Pass journal entries for above transactions in the books of the company.

10. *Amreli oil Ltd. Issued on 1-1-1998 10,000 8 % mortgage debentures of Rs.100 each to raise debt capital on the following terms.*

   (1)   Debentures will be redeemed at 10 % premium.

   (2)   Debentures will be redeemed on 31-12-2004 with an option to debentures holders to choose any of the following modes of redemption

   (1)   Issue of equity share of Rs.10 each at a premium of Rs.2 per share

Or

   (2)   Issue of 10 % preference shares of Rs.100 each at 20 % premium.

Or

(3) Issue of *6 %* new debentures of *Rs.100* each at *10 %* discount.

Or

(4) Cash payment on redemption.

Different debentures holders exercised different options as per the details given below:

Holders of *4200* debentures accepted equity shares.

Holders of *3000* debentures accepted preference shares.

Holders Of *1800* debentures accepted new debentures

Holders of *1000* debentures accepted cash.

Write the necessary journal entries at the time of issue and redemption debentures.

☐ LATEST EXAMINATION ☐

---

11. Surya Lts " issued *5000 8 %* debentures of *Rs.100* each at *10 %* premium and redeemed at par. Pass the necessary journal entries in the books of the Company (Narration is not necessary) *(MARCH-2009)*

12. Gayatri Ltd issued debentures of *Rs.900000* at a discount of *10 %* At the end of every year a sum of *Rs.300000* is to be redeemed out of this amount and is to be paid. To debentures holders Prepare a Debentures discount account in the books of the Company. *(JULY 2009)*

13. On **1-1-2003** Birva Ltd. Issued **10000 12 %** debentures of **Rs.100** each at a discount of **10 %** All the debentures are to be redeemed after six year at a premium **10 %** Pass the necessary journal entries in the books of the Company for the issue and redemption of debentures (without narration). **(JULY 2009)**

14. On **1-4-2000 50,000 10 %** debenture of **Rs.100** each were issued at **5%**discount which were redeemed on **31-3-2006** at **10 %** premium. Pass the necessary journal entries in the books of the company for the issue and redemption of debenture without narration. **(MARCH-2010)**

15. On **1-7-2005** Prarthna ltd. Issued **6000 9%** debentures of **Rs.100** each at par The debentures are to be redeemed on **30-6-2009** at **Rs.115** per debentures pass the necessary journal entries in the books of the company for the issue and redemption of debentures.

(JULY 2010, MARCH-2013)

16. On **1**st april 2004 avishkar ltd. Issued **15000 6.5%** convertible debenture of **Rs.100** each at **5%** discount as per terms of debenture all the debentures will be converted into equity shares of **Rs.10** each at a premium of **25%** after 4 years.

On **1**st april 2008 debentures were converted into equity shares as per the agreed terms. Write the necessary journal entries in the books of the co.

OR

*Karnavati textiles ltd. Issued **9 %** debentures of **Rs.100** each on the following terms.*

   *a) **30,000** debentures at **Rs.95**.*

   *b) Issued **4500** debentures of **Rs.100** each against purchase of machinery of **Rs.5,00,000**.*

   *c) **Issued 3500** debentures of **Rs.100** each as collateral security against loan of **Rs.250000** pass journal entries for above transactions in the book of the company. **(MARCH-2011)***

17.   *Umiya Scrap ltd issued **50,000 10 %** debentures of **Rs.100** each debentures are issued at **5%** discount and redeemed at par. Write the necessary journal entries in the bokks of the company at the time of issue and redemption of debentures. **(JULY 2011)***

18.   *Ravi ltd.issued 7 % debentures each of **Rs.100** with following conditions : **(MARCH-2012)***

   *1. **Rs.94** per debentures 30,000 debentured with cash.*

   *2. 7,000 debentures each of **Rs.100,** are given to trader with an exchange of purchase of machinery worth **Rs.8,00,000**.*

   *3. 11,000debentures as a collateral security, each of **Rs.100,** given to bank for loan worth **Rs.9,00,000**.*

19.   *Kamal ltd. Issued **10,000 9 %** debentures of **Rs.100** each at **10 %** premium on **01-04-03** and redeemed at par on **30-3-09** pass the journal entry in the books of the Kamal ltd. Narration is not necessary. **(MARCH-2012)***

20. On 1-1- 2001 Banwari Ltd. Issued **3,000** 8 % debentures of **Rs.100 each at a discount of 6%** Accounting year of the company ends on **31 st December** The debentures were redeemed asunder:

Debentures were redeemed as under :

Date	Numbers of debentures redeemed
31-12-2001	1200
31-12-2002	900
31-12-2003	600
31-12-2004	300

Prepare a debentures discount account in the books of the company. **(JULY 2012)**

21. Issued **40,000** debentures of **Rs.100 each on 1-1-98** at par which were redeemed on **1-1-2005** at **10 %** premium.

Pass the necessary journal entries in the books of the company for the issue and redemption of debentures.

(JULY 2012)

22. on **1-4-2001** Bharat limited issued **7500 6.5 %** convertible debentures of **Rs.100** each at **5 %** discount. As per the terms of the issue of debentures. All debenture will converted into enquiry share of **Rs.10.** Each at a premium of **25%** after **4** years. On **1-4-2005** debentures were converted into enquiry share as per the agreed terms write the journal entries. **(MARCH-2013)**

23. on **1-1-2001** Modi zerox ltd. Issued **8000 11%** debentures of **Rs.100** each at a discount of **5%.** All the *debentures are to be redeemed after six years at a premium of 10%Pass the necessary journal entries in the books of the company.particulars not necessary. (MARCH-2014)*

24. *Balaram cement ltd. Issued 9 % debentures of Rs.100 each on the following terms :*

1) *40000 debentures at Rs.95.*

2) *Issued 9000 debentures of Rs.100each against. Purchase of machinery of Rs. 10,00,000.*

3) *Issued 7000 debentures of Rs.100 each as collateral security against, loan of Rs.5,00,000.*

Pass journal entries for the above transaction.

(MARCH-2014)

............×××××××××............

Chapter : 5

"Analysis of Financial Statements"

☐ THEORY SECTION ☐

Q:-1 State the utility or objective of financial statements.

* ❖ *Published financial statements are relied upon by the public at large and increase the creditability of the company.*
* ❖ *Share holders get more information about the company where by increasing their level of confidence in the company.*
* ❖ *Financial statements add to the reputation of company.*
* ❖ *Financial statements give information about performance, progress and position to all stakeholders.*
* ❖ *Lenders lending money to company and creditors supplying goods to company get information useful to them from the financial statements.*

Q:- 2 State the objectives of financial statement analysis

Analysis is also made to ascertain to what extent the requirements for preparation of financial statement are complied with these objectives are :

* ❖ *Whether provision of Compares Act complied with or not.*

❖ *To ascertain true and fair profit of the company and to determine income tax liability based on that.*

❖ *When shares of the company are listed at stock exchange whether guidelines and requirements laid down by SEBI and other controlling authorities are complied with.*

❖ *To help management in framing different policies.*

❖ *Apart from above, the objectives with different parties are interested in financial statements analysis are discussed earlier.*

Q:- 3 State limitations of financial statements:

A company prepares profit and loss account and balance sheet at the end of year. Such financial statements also have certain limitations these limitations are as under :

1) ***Accuracy*** *:sometimes perfect information's are not given in financial statements. So the statements do not show the exact position of the business that is why. Less accuracy is indicated in the financial statements.*

2) ***Values of assets*** *: generally, fixed assets are shown in balance sheet at their depreciated values. However, its market values are different moreover, balance sheet cannot show usefulness or efficiency of these assets. Method of providing depreciation is also subjective at times.*

3) ***Inflationary condition*** *: under inflationary condition the values of assets constantly increase. Because of less depreciation is provided profit appears to be more.*

4) Efficiency of management : *efficiency of management can't be directly presented in such statements generally, efficiency of management is an important factor affecting profitability or business however, profit and loss account can't depict this factor on the face of it.*

5) Valuation of stock : *financial statements may not show proper picture if method of valuation of stock is not appropriate.*

6) Other parties : *financial statements are both prepared from the viewpoints of all stakeholders associated with the enterprise usually, they are prepared from the viewpoint of shareholders and management.*

7) Other factors : *many external factors like policies of competitors general economic condition political factors and monopolistic condition affect the economic position of business as a result the finical statements may not present true or proper financial position.*

8) Liabilities : *the balance sheet of the company does not to disclose all the liabilities of business e.g amount of gratuity payable to their employees and as a consequence, the balance sheet falls to show the true financial position of the company.*

Q.4 State limitations of financial statement analysis :

1) Less accuracy : *if the financial statements which are analyzed are not prepared with accuracy, the analysis and interpretations based on such analysis can't be reliable :*

2) Government rules : *changing government rules and controls affect preparation of financial statements. This will have its effect on analysis financial statements also.*

3) Accounting standards *: limitations of alternative accounting treatments inbuilt and permitted by the accounting standards also affect the analysis of financial statements*

4) Companies act : *changes in provisions of companies act also have an effect on quality of financial analysis.*

5) Analyzing : *efficiency and maturity of professionals analyzing financial statements could also become a limitations of analysis :*

Q:-5 Write short note : Common Size Statements.

*These statements are prepares to know percentage of each of assets to total assets and percentage of each element of expenses as percentage of total sales. Such statements are also known as **100** percentage statements.*

Common size statements are also useful in comparing financial position of two compares While analyzing balance sheet, each asset as a % of total assets and each liability as a % of total liabilities is calculated Similarly. In analyzing P & L A/c each item of Exp and income is calculated as % of total sales.

*For Example cash is **7 %** of total assets and the same is **10 %** in case of some other company. In Means that the liquidity position of other company is better.*

Thus, Common-size statements can tell us about how much difference is there and where the difference lies, However, to know about the ideal position and about the reasons for difference, detailed investigation necessary.

............×××××××××............